To Evely,
Thank,
and the talent we [share]

R.P.C.G. Moore

DEDICATED TO YOU

DEDICATED TO YOU

B.J.C.G. Moore

Copyright © 2007 by B.J.C.G. Moore.

Library of Congress Control Number: 2007903196
ISBN: Hardcover   978-1-4257-5917-9
             Softcover   978-1-4257-5904-9

All rights reserved. No part of this book may be reproduced or transmitted in any form or by any means, electronic or mechanical, including photocopying, recording, or by any information storage and retrieval system, without permission in writing from the copyright owner.

This is a work of fiction. Names, characters, places and incidents either are the product of the author's imagination or are used fictitiously, and any resemblance to any actual persons, living or dead, events, or locales is entirely coincidental.

This book was printed in the United States of America.

To order additional copies of this book, contact:
Xlibris Corporation
1-888-795-4274
www.Xlibris.com
Orders@Xlibris.com

39275

CONTENTS

1. All the way 11
2. A Lotta Yesterdays Ago 13
3. What Did Jesus Write 15
4. Be still and Listen 17
5. Born and Die 19
6. Church or Bar 21
7. God's Creation 23
8. Shelter From The Storm 26
9. A Stewardess 28
10. The Future 30
11. The Saintly Mother Teresa 32
12. Basirah Taha 33
13. Bernadette Augustine 35
14. Friends 37
15. Billy the Kid 39
16. Mary Koonce Patterson 42
17. Diana 44
18. Ira Woods 45
19. Mr. B. 47
20. Eyes and Ears 49
21. God's Wonder 51
22. I See I Know I will 53
23. I wish you 56
24. Mama 58
25. I don't want to be here 61
26. Georgia Street 63
27. My Friend 66
28. My Men 67
29. Pig Pen to the Potter's House 69
30. The Final Poem 71
31. The Message or the Messenger 72

32. Thelma Elizabeth Henderson 75
33. A Woman for every situation 77
34. My Song My Prayer 79
35. My Testimony 80
36. Over the Rainbow 83
37. People 85
38. Reason and Season 87
39. Satan wants his job back 89
40. The Lie 92
41. Worlds Ends 95

NORMA J. (Habibah) MOORE/DAVIS

DEDICATED TO YOU

You are my last, but not least
By any stretch of the imagination
You, like the many wonders of the world
Are one of God's greatest creations

B.J.C.G.M.

Dedicated to you Norma J. (Habibah) Moore/Davis

This is compilation of works, also dedicated to friends, and acquaintances that I have met over the years of my life. So many different people, races, creeds and genders sharing so many of the same issues. So many similar issues in health, personal and religious problems. Problems with their spouses, their jobs, their children, their weight and their finances. Wars, world hunger, cancer. Aids and so many, many things that one can't even begin to imagine.

One of the greatest words in any dictionary, in any language is hello. Hello is the beginning of many great relationships of all kind, love affairs, and business deals, bonding of nations, and mending hurt feelings and clearing up misunderstanding.

A sincere hello followed by a real conversation putting all agendas on the table could prevent many misunderstandings and conflicts.

A sincere hello could make people look at each other as human beings, and see that under All of our pretenses, isms, bigotry and hate we are more a like than we can imagine.

All the way

People keep talking about where you brought me from
I keep talking about where you are taking me to
Since you have forgiven and forgotten where I've been
I am just praising you for bringing me through

Looking back, I remember many days and nights
That I couldn't remember what I done or said
Each day I love and praise you more
Because without you I could have ended up dead

I know I wasn't the best son in the world
But you let my parents live long enough to see
How you have cleaned me up and turned me around
And what you have made of me

I am so glad I listened when you chose my mate
Although that didn't make a man or husband of me
But through honest prayers I stuck it out
Now I know how wonderful a marriage can be

I didn't know anything about being a father
But you gave me beautiful fruit from my seeds
Thank you for being the wonderful God you are
My mate and I did our best with the deeds

The life long job you provided for me
Wasn't the best, but it was enough
Many times I wanted to throw up my hands and quit
But you were with me when the times were tough

Thank you Lord, Now all of that is behind me
Now I can devote all of my time and praise to you
While the world look back to where you brought me from
I look straight ahead to where you are taking me to

Teach me what to say to the spectators
Who constantly try to remind me of my past
Help me show them, that what's done for Christ
Those are the only things that will last

As the world remembers where I have been
And all of the thing I have been through
I keep my eyes on the prize
Because I am going all the way with you

Thank you Lord for this step up the ladder
Please humble me more and more each day
Make my thoughts and deeds more like yours
For that, Dear Lord, I daily pray

Now Lord I am in it for the long haul
Through the storms and temptations, come what may
I wouldn't take nothing for my journey now
I am going with you all the way

A Lotta Yesterdays Ago

I remember when I thought I was hot stuff
But now I am moving kinda slow
There wasn't much I wouldn't do
But that was a lot of yesterdays ago

I used to work ten to twelve hours a day
Six and seven days a week
But that was when I was young and strong
And my body was slim and sleek

I used to party the entire weekend
Get tired, not me, oh no
And I would get angry if I missed one party
But that was a lota yesterdays ago

I had many real good jobs back then
But I couldn't save one dime
But money was never an object
I just never had enough time

My hair, my clothes and shoes were priority
And a lota money to keep my car up
Because every time anyone made a toast
I tried to be there to raise my cup

Thank God I didn't like trouble
As fast as I was traveling, you would never know
I could have ended up in jail or dead
A lota yesterdays ago

If the bartender poured it, I drank it
Scotch, vodka, wine and gin
Nights when I was not too drunk I prayed
For I knew I was living in sin

But everything I did was not all bad
And especially if I didn't drink too much
Some Sundays I would put on my dark glasses
And sit in the back of the church

I smoked cigarettes by the carton
Drinked anything that would make me drunk
Thank you O God for loving me
And not letting me get hooked on junk

Looking back I remembered my mothers' prayers
Praying for things she didn't even know
Now, I realized she knew much more than me
But that was a lota yesterdays ago

When I look at the youth today
Some are into cars, sneakers, leather and gold chains
But every generation has their own hell
Which will pass away and won't mean a thing?

I just hope their mothers, like mine
Stay in touch with God in prayer
And make sure daily that their children know
No matter what, she and God loves them and care

Dear Lord, I thank you for the journey
Why you brought me through, I don't know
For without you I was hell bound
But that was a lota yesterdays ago

Now that I am living for Jesus
I have found a joy that the world should know
That I was seeking in the parties and bottles
A lota yesterdays ago

What Did Jesus Write

Was this woman not born an innocent baby?
On the same earth as you and I
Was she born a sinful woman?
Or was she contaminated, by whom and how

Should she be killed because she is a woman?
Her sin, did she commit them alone
Did she sin with you, you or you?
Then shouldn't you too be stoned

Is she guilty of stealing?
A few barley loaves of bread
Because maybe she was hungry
Or to see to it that her family was fed

Or maybe she took in a wayward traveler
Out of the elements, a storm or the cold
Thinking he or she was sent by God the Father
With a blessing for her soul

Or maybe she lied for no reason
Or helped a friend out on the Sabbath day
A day that is set aside by God
To rest, to be thankful and pray

Or maybe she left her husbands bed
To share the bed with another
Not caring that the other man was her kin
For he was her husbands brother

Or maybe she did not aid the sick
Or turned someone in need away
Or she did not rebuke the devil
Or maybe led someone's child astray

There are so many things we stoners are guilty of
Are we sure we are not guilt in the father's sight
If we know for sure that we are guilt less
Why walk away when Jesus started to write

If you know that you have not sinned
And by no means done anything wrong
Then you should be delegated
To cast the very first stone

The woman could sense this man was special
She just knew that he was precious in Gods sight
She knew this must be the savior
But what did Jesus write

Did he write you stoners name her sin?
Do you know that the accusers are true?
Are you 100% sure that she is guilty
Did she do these unforgivable deeds with you?

If her crime is punishable by death
Should she be punished alone?
If you committed these sin with her
Shouldn't you too be stoned?

Be still and Listen

Oh Lord! What is my purpose?
Why did you put me on earth?
Why me of all people
Why did you let my mother give me birth?

My life seems so meaningless
What did you make me to do?
My Bible tells me to be still
To wait and listen to you

My mother taught me to love and trust you
Before I knew what love and trust was about
Now I know that there is no one greater than you
About that there is no doubt

Lord I try to teach little children
To listen to what the elderly have to say
I commune with the sick and shut in
And I never forget to pray

Lord I want to be a good disciple
To be still and listen to you
To be a kind, loving, fisher of men
And do what ever you want me to do

My Bible says if I fast and pray
Be still and do your will
You will give me the desires of my heart
You will fight my battles, if I be still

You calmed my stormy seas
Sent my prodigal children back home
Make sure my barrel is never empty
And promises never to leave me alone

O Lord thank you for letting me be born
Keep me still so that I can hear you
When you say well-done my faithful disciple
When I've done what you put me on earth to do

Born and Die

The two most important days in one's life
Is when they are born and die
And at neither time are they aware
Of what is happening or why

Mother did the toil and labor
But you are still the star
Mother is just glad it's over
You take the bows not even knowing who you are

You don't even know how blessed you are
You have been given the greatest gift on earth
Life, health, wealth and love
When God gave you his breath

He gave you the parents he designed for you
A world of opportunity to choose
Make the most of everything and everyone around you
You don't have one moment to lose

Many people live for money
Material things fortune and fame
Not realizing those things too are gifts
All in Jesus name

You don't realize it until it's too late
You only have God's breath and time
You can amass a whole world of things
Like you were born, you will die without a dime

Enjoy every minute God gives you
Don't waste time crying and grieving
Spend your time producing, loving, and caring
And be careful about the legacy you are leaving

A good word, good thoughts, good deeds
The examples you leave in this life
Teaching one person to be thankful and rejoice
In the midst of stress and strife

All too soon you will realize
That your time is running out
Then you will begin to appreciate your gift
As you realize what your gift is all about

All of the things you acquired in your youth
Fortune and fame is slipping away
As you start loosing your hair, teeth and memory
And personal control with every birthday

Everyday is more precious
As you pass that three score and ten
As you think of the many things you would do
If you could live your life over again

As your knees weaken and your back bends
You are slowly approaching the grave
Your prayers and thoughts are more constant
As you thank God for his breath he gave

Finally all of your earthly functions stop
Once again you are the star
No more what did you do on earth
And only God knows where you are

Dedicated to and inspired by
Reverend Sheila Pigford

Church or Bar

Dear Lord while just sitting and listening
To the conversation of a so called friend
That was equating the bars to the churches
But Lord we are not going to let you die again

Maybe O Lord we have become careless
Not lifting your name up in praise
We are not showing the world what a great God you are
By not going out into the hedges and the highways

True the bars are always crowded
But so is the road to hell
In the mornings their souls are troubled
But with us, all with our souls are well

In the bars they pay for what they get
With money that is needed for clothing and rent
Dear Lord you give us all everything we get
And you only ask for ten percent

Now Lord it is time for us to go out
And show the world how truly great you are
And tell the world very loud and clear
And show them the difference in the church and the bar

The wine they drink just dull the brain
And make men loud, ignorant, and profane
The wine we drink is a perpetual memory
Uplifting the blood in Jesus name

Yes Lord it's time we got serious
Like our ancestors from the past
And show the church and the bar
That only what's done for Christ will last

But our hearts and souls are the issue
Not the church or the bar
If we really have Jesus Christ planted in our hearts
We can have church wherever we are

Just remember God made the sticks and stones
That made the buildings wherever you are
God safely placed you here on this earth
And coming back for you, either in the church or in the bar

No Lord, we won't let the world kill you again
You are in our hearts where ever we are
We are going out into the hedges and highways
And show the world the difference in the church and the bar

Yes Lord we have got to show the bars
That we love you, and our neighbors so much
And that there is an uplifting peace we find
Whenever we are in church

An uplifting that won't let you down
That will make you shout wherever you are
That is something that money can't buy
And something you won't find in the bar

Dedicated to and inspired by a devoted woman of God,
an Educator, Mother with a voice that you could
listen to twenty-four hours a day

Mrs. Carla Booth Hines

God's Creation

Scientist says that earth is an accident
The results of a supernatural blast
But I believe what my Bible says
God is the first word and the last

Before God spoke there was no scientist
No blast, just nothingness
God spoke, and made everything in six days
Then he took a rest

What blast would know where to place an ocean?
Or where to stop a sea
Or how high to make a mountain
Or where to plant a tree

No blast could make a perfect garden
With all species of animals that would mind
All kinds of fruits and vegetables
To sustain the life of mankind

How can a blast make a man?
Without blemish or sin, that's odd
When men was then, and always will be
Made in the image of God

How would everything be watered?
Man the animals and grain
When man and animal alike
Had never heard of rain

A blast did not even create the serpent
That helped to break the bond between God and man
That coerced man and woman to sin
Back when the world began

What kind of blast would have cared?
If the soul of man was lost
That would create the perfect lamb
To come down and pay the cost

Yes scientist says it was a blast
That created you and me
And that we are just part of the evolution
From the jungle or from the sea

Scientist says that we and earth
Is just a mysterious whim
I wonder if scientist really doesn't know
That God made the earth and him

I wonder if scientist really thinks
That a blast created men with the different hues
Different finger prints and talents for everyone
The rainbow red, green, yellows and blues

Did the blast create the different languages?
That is spoken by the different races of men
The hate, the greed and covertness
That would lead the world to sin

So scientist you call it phenomenon
Call it mistake or mysterious blast
But My God made this world with a word
He is the first word and the last

I wonder if scientist and the blast
Knew then as well as now
The many wants and needs of a man
And what to do for man and how

Read your Bible and trust God
All of you young boys and girls
If scientist knew how then, they know how now
Believe me; they would make another world

So let scientist call it phenomenon
Even call if a puff of smoke
There would be no scientist or a world
If God had never stepped out and spoke

Shelter From The Storm

Time, take me back
Back to the days of yore
Back to the ark of safety
Back to the God of Noah

Where no sin or evil can touch me
Leaning on my saviors welcoming arms
My God speaks to the winds and waves
And rides upon the storm

There is no place you can run
There is no place to hide
Choose your shelter here and now
There is safety on the Lord's side

Bow your heads silently for our neighbors
For our savior to ease their suffering and pain
Just think, it could have been you or me
Devoured by that storm and rain

Loosing all of their earthly possessions
The things they gave their heart and soul for
Loosing homes, jobs, and loved ones
Awareness, some not knowing who or where they are

Many are stumbling around in a daze
Going to sleep, waking up in shock
They built their houses on sinking sand
Instead of Christ the solid rock

We have got to get closer to God
Talk to him, and listen to him every day
Tell the Lord all of our problems
And listen to what he has to say

There are storms and rains in every life
Just lean on God's everlasting arm
Just turn it all over to Jesus
He is the shelter in the time of a storm

He is your protection from life's ups and downs
He protects you from all hurt and harm
Be still let him fight your battles
Let him be your shelter from the storm

Don't despair the storm is not God
God is your shelter, he is tried and true
God will give you so much more
Than any storm can ever take from you

Dedicated to my stewardess Sisters of St. Paul A.M.E. Church

A Stewardess

I am one of God's stewardesses
On this old ship of Zion bound for glory
I am so proud to stand here for the Lord
To tell you my wonderful story

Of how God saved my soul one day
When I was hopelessly lost
How he sent his only begotten son
To die on Calvary's rugged cross

How he picked me up out of the mire
When I were lost and sinking down
He stopped me and ordered my steps
And he turned my life around

How he fed me when I was hungry
Kept watch nightly over my bed
Brought my prodigal children back home
Did all of the things he said

After going to church Sunday after Sunday
Just sitting quietly in the pew
I prayed Lord you've been so good to me
What would you have me do?

He said get up be a stewardess
Go out; compel my sheep to come in
Welcome those wayward sinners
Tell them to turn away from sin

Visit the sick and the shut in
Visit the prisons and the jails
Tell those inmates to get their tickets indorsed
Before the old ship of Zion sails

Tell those children to honor their parents
Tell the parents don't use their children as tools
Because letting those children go astray
Is being neglectively, ungodly and cruel

Be a good kind godly stewardess
For you do not know when or how
That ship will come to take you
To your heavenly home by and by

The Future

Mom/Dad I am the future
I am what your tomorrow will bring
All of that is up to you
Make me great, make me everything

I am your seed
Plant me, water me, and nurture me
Make me whatever you want me to be
Make me a weed, crab grass or a bush
Or you can make me a mighty tree

Mom/Dad I am your gift from God
And God is going to reward you
By the values you put in me
And by the works I do

I need leadership, training and guidance
So steer me, show me the way
You have been where I am going
Teach me to be thankful, and to pray

I could be President, Preacher or teacher
A Doctor, Lawyer or Judge
When you see me falling back
Give me a parental nudge

I could be a singer, dancer or a scientist
My future right now, is in your hands
Whether or not I am a useful and productive
loving, caring, God fearing woman or man

Yes, you have got to shape me and mold me
That will be long days and toilsome nights
But all of that is what it will take
If I am to make your future bright

I can just imaging that will be a task
But every road has crooks and turns
But the trek is only as hard as we make it
But that too we will have to learn

Yes, Mom/Dad I am your tomorrow
It is up to you how grand it will be
How you prepare me for my future right now
Is what you can expect your future to be?

The Saintly Mother Teresa
A Light in the Window

You are a light in yonder window
A heart that is full of care
To the helpless, hopeless stranger
There is love and warmth in there

There is shelter for the homeless
Arms for the unwanted child
You are something special for everyone
If nothing more than a smile

To you it never mattered
About the titles and prizes you won
Your heart and souls satisfaction was
The knowledge of a job well done

Although your light down here below
Has finally come to an end
The flicker will glow in the needy's mind
As they come around the bend

That light in yonder window
Shone steadfast and bright for years
Aided the hurt, the hungry, the forgotten
And wiped away many tears

Good-by light in yonder window
Thank you for a job well done
You are a flicker from a greater light
You are a spark from the son

Basirah Taha
My Shero

Today I am over come with joy
My face is radiant with a smile
For she not only is my Shero
Greatest of all she is my child

She was born in the month of many greats
Face flushed as a newly ripe cherry
Born on a late Monday afternoon
During the month of February

Born a few fractions from perfection
But that makes her all the more great
Eager to tackle the world from birth
Too much to do, no time to wait

She was very shy and retiring
So she made reading her great escape
She could slip into and out of worlds
Like the opening and closing of the drapes

She could slip through her looking glass
And be whatever she wanted to be
A doctor, lawyer, or an astronaut
Or the beauty, the world was waiting to see

But far too soon she realized
That promises and mirrors could break
So she had to go out and face the world
With trials, errors and mistakes

She struggled, studied and worked real hard
Was advised, but never done as she was told
She knew she had to go beyond boundaries
Before she could ever reach her goal

She said if it can be done
Then why in the world can't I
If any one on this earth has done it
I too am going to give it my best try

Still everyday there is a new challenge
There is always one more thing yet to do
Once she takes the plunge to jump in
She is going to see the job through

She may never climb a mountain, or stop the drugs traffic
Or for the many different illnesses, find a cure
But wherever she goes, you'll know she was there
For she always leaves her signature

Now you know why I walk around like a Peacock
With a smile that I am proud to show
For she not only, is my child
I am so proud to say, that she is my Shero

Bernadette Augustine
Circle President and My Friend
The circle

Many of you come to church when you want to
If you feel like it you say Amen
The preacher preach, the choir sings
You are not moved without or within

If you want to you walk around the table
Tithing, giving God his due
Can you honestly say to yourself
That money is all that God has given you

What about the time God gave you
The life and that talent he gave you too
When you walk up and give God money
Are you really giving him his due?

We all can't sing like angels
Nor can we all preach like Paul
But there is one thing for certain
God gave a talent to us all

Once in a while you can give a testimony
Or go to the altar, kneel and pray
Say a kind word to a visitor
That might make them join your church some day

When a club or a board in your church
Seems to be slipping, or is not too sound
Join them, prop them up
Don't just gossip, trying to tear them down

Now we the Florida, Alabama, African,
Caribbean circle, are getting older
We have slowed down in a great way
Still we love our elders and shut ins
And pray for them everyday

When we can, we go and visit the elderly
Read the Bible, and Pray a prayer
You should see the smiles and their tears
Knowing that their church remembers them and care

Since we are the only geological club left
Join us wherever you are from, we don't mind
Our main goal is to serve God
And to be friend all of man kind

We pray a special prayer for our president
Ms. Bernadette Augustine and her stick-to-itiveness
Who says we will just keep holding on and praying?
The circle will once again be a great success

So if you are just sitting in the church
Not clapping your hands or stomping your feet
Just come on out and join the circle
Your reward will be O so sweet

Friends

I made a friend the other day
While traveling on the bus
We hit it off so well together
The other riders did not know what to think of us

We were talking to each other
As if we had met years ago
Talking about nothing in particular
Not caring, nor did we know

Nothing at all about backgrounds
Not caring about sides of the track
Just knowing, we were having a great time
The way true friends should act

We weren't concerned with politics
Nor did we care who won the war
Just appreciating all of God's creations
And marveling at advancing so far

We did speak of racial differences
One of today's greatest shames
The blacks, the white, the rich, the poor
And who, or what, is to blame

Suddenly our conversation changed
It was not carefree any longer
As we spoke of people living homelessly
And children dying of hunger

Then we spoke of yesterday
When there was faith, trust and love
Of friends befriending all people
And trusting in God above

We spoke of today's children
O God, and above everything else
Children having children too young
It's like children raising themselves

It was such a pleasant bus ride
We didn't know where the time had gone
Meeting people for the first time
Has a reward of its own

The bus came to my new friends stop
Our brief meeting came to and end
We laughed and talked and came close to tears
But that's what you call a friend

As my friend stepped of the bus
This thought came to mind
I did not get a number or address
And true friends are hard to find

I looked at the empty seat beside me
Unaware I started to grin
Of course the seat had to be vacated
To be filled by my next new friend

Billy the Kid

Let me tell you about bad boy Billy
People don't want to hear of the good he did
Because he was betrayed by his weakness
It is said that he was worst than Billy the Kid

Later, for the wars he prevented
And the jobless he took of the streets
Still the world was far more concerned about
What happened on his sheets?

One thing, he gave over looked, qualified people
A chance to work in high places
For that, they said he turned his back on his own
And the position he holds, he disgraces

They said he never deserved such a position
Because he was born and raised in the ghetto
And there were too many of the right people
That deserved that position more

They said he done so many unthinkable things
That it is impossible to believe he did
They said he should have been kicked of his position
For he was worst than the original Billy the Kid

They called him the first black president
Because he tried to treat all people right
He acted like he cared about all people
Jews, Gentiles, Black and white

Everyday there was a new criticism
At the very least his job was very hard
Whatever Billy done, they said it was wrong
They called him everything but a child of God

He held that position 2,920 days
Working like his predecessors from sun to sun
But most people blotted out 2, 919 of them
And of all of his days they remembered just one

They said as a man he was a womanizer
In a lower position he was a scandelizer
They kept him and his life under a microscope
They said he was also a demoralizer

Just like everything done everywhere
He was being a man without a thought
He done nothing that hasn't been done before
But it was him, and he got caught

For many years officials have turned their heads
To fornicating, lying, murder and stealing
Not to mention mistreating the under dog
Backstabbing, broken promises and double dealing

So many things are covered up in the big house
Anyone could name a hundred and two
But it's according to who you are
And getting caught, doing whatever you do

Billy was not caught, doing anything
But he admitted telling a lie
Most of the posse's tried to kill him
They said that Billy the Kid deserved to die

Billy asked the world to forgive him
His family, preachers, teachers, Elders and such
But the righteous Tele-Evangelist said
He and those forgivers should be kicked out of the church

Those Holy Rollers never read about King David
Of his covertness and thrill
Because he could, he defiled Bathsheba
And too, he had her husband killed

The world expected Mrs. Kid
To pack her bags and leave him
But Mrs. Kid was more woman than most
She would not go along with them

Billy and Mrs. Kid wrote books, and went on TV
Many people missed a whole days pay
Just to buy books and watch TV
To see, hear and read what they might say

They didn't care what the book was about
Nor what they went on TV to say
They were looking for a verbatim description
Of what went on that day

Billy blew his horn on TV
Said in his youth, smoked some weed
I wonder just what you would hear
If other officials confessed their deeds

I wonder if the history books will record
Some of the many good things he done
Or will they ignore the 2,919 days
And just record that one

Mary Koonce Patterson

Council Woman

A very loyal and devoted politician. One of the nicest persons in the world to call a friend. A choir director, lover of children, a beautiful wife and mother, she is always there when ever a political problem comes up. Thank you Mary, And I thank God for letting you be a part of mine and my family's life.

Take me where, Tell me when, Show me how

Lord I have always been a little pushy
But that, you already know
Still I wait for you to tell me when and how
And show me where to go

Now I am a politician, on this highway of life
I give all the thanks and praise to you
You are the first and last president
Thanks for making me a part of that too

For I have always wanted to help my fellow man
But I never knew exactly where or why
You, through politics, have opened that door
Now Lord please show me how

I have met many politicians that are corrupt
Evil ungodly and full of sin
That is why I beg you daily, O Lord
Tell me what to do and when

I have never campaigned with back stabbing lies
I try to be as honest as I can
And I always pray that what ever the position
It goes to the most qualified woman or man

I know I can't save every stray child
Nor help all of the seniors and the poor
But with your help I will do my best
O Lord I know only you can do more

I know I can't clean up every street
Nor straighten the heart of every cop on the beat
But dear Lord I know you have the answer
And a solution to every challenge I meet

I don't want to change the unchangeable
Nor do I want to fret about it
But until I do some good and make a difference
I promise you I won't quit

Thank you O Lord for making me a politician
I learned so many things I never knew
How better to serve you and my community
And all praises are due to you

There don't seem to be enough hours in a day
To finish each project I start or try
But take me where, tell me when
And dear Lord please show me how

I can't straighten out every class room
Nor stop a teen from stealing a car
Nor stop the disgraceful drug traffic
Nor close down a bar

But for what ever position I am elected
Dear Lord I will do my best
Tell me when, how and what I can do
And I know you will do the rest

Dear Lord I am a politician in life's arena
Take me, tell me, and show me what you will have me do
And I will give my family, my Church and East Orange my best
And give all the thanks and praise to you

Diana

Diana you are and always will be a princess
Oh, but the price you paid
The more you tried to make England shine
The more they rained on your parade

They took you in, an innocent babe
They matured you over night
Your dreams of a life of love and happiness
Turned out to be a nightmare of fright

They tried to destroy the beauty in you
But forever it will show
Though they rained on your parade
To so many you will always be their rainbow

Your love and care for humankind
Was as true as the colors of the rainbow
Though your deeds on earth is done
In each rainy life, your love will show

To us death is so untimely
But God knows when each angel must go
But for every rainy life you touched
They will remember you, their rainbow

Forever when we see a rainbow
Our hearts will say a silent prayer
For within our heart we will always know
Diana, you are there

Dedicated to Ira Woods a blessed Organist, Educator, and I was fortunate enough to hear him preach his ordaining sermon. God bless you and I thank him for allowing me to be one of the people to sing under your directions

Ira Woods

Welcome back IRA WOODS we missed you
You came when we needed you the most
We know that God leads and guide you
For you were sent by the Holy Ghost

Though we never say, "I Love You"
Nor show you how much we care
Examine the contents of our hearts
You will find that you are there

Too we appreciate your professionalism
Though we constantly gripe and mourn
But the mere thought of loosing you
Leaves us empty and forlorn

Yes you came when we needed someone
Thank God he sent you our way
You are always in our thoughts and heart
Whenever we kneel and pray

No one pleases everyone
Still we try, we do the very best we can
Only God makes perfect angels
That's something all believers understand

We know that you are a man of God
For we can feel his presence in you
And no matter what obstacles you face
We know that God will see you through

Welcome back is a common phrase
We love you, is mere words too
But we are going to show you how much
By our sincerity in the things we do

Mr. B.

Thank you for your time and patience Mr. B
You have been a wonderful friend
Month after month I looked forward to
Your boyish smile or grin

Though our monthly meetings weren't a gaiety
Nor is it something I will always treasure
No matter how unpleasant some of them were
Seeing you was always a pleasure

You never looked down your nose at us
To made us feel like beggars or such
You acted like each one of us mattered
To me that meant so much

To many, welfare is just a job
To earn a check, they have to do their part
But you treated each client with care
And concern, from the heart

There were times the recipients were nasty
Very abusive and unkind
You handled each situation professionally
You never seemed upset, nor did you mind

From experience, I know your job is trying
And that trying to be kind, will wear you out
Keep your gloves on, keep up your defense
You will surely win the bout

The very first time I met you, you said
Something I will remember my whole life through
"As long as you respect me as a human being
I will give that same respect to you"

Those simple words meant so much to me
Something the simple ear might not understand
In my minds eye that made you ten feet tall
Heads above the average man

Mr. B. I have the utmost love and respect for you
You are a wonderful human being
There is a special place in my heart for you
I hold you in the highest esteem

And for the short time I have known you
You proved every word to be true
I pray our paths won't cross this particular way again
Whether or not, I thank you, and God bless you

Eyes and Ears

Don't look at me with your ears
That's why God gave you eyes
The ears can no more see truth
Than the eyes can hear lies

When you tell the ears that you are green
Then green is what you are
But you cannot tell the eyes that you are the Sun
When the eyes see that you are a star

You can tell the ears I love you
But the eye sees what you do
The eye sees your action
Is that really what I mean to you?

If you tell the ears you'll always be there
Through the thick and the thin
And if you are there, you hide in the crowd
And no one even know that you are a friend

If someone tells you that I am not trust worthy
And your eyes see that they are lies
Are you going to keep believing your ears?
Or will you start believing your eyes

Don't miss your greatest friendship ever?
The best friend you might have ever had
Because you are looking through someone's mouth
That would be a sin, and oh so sad

Just remember the life of Jesus
His life, the blood shed and the tears
Crucified, not for what was seen by the eyes
But by what was heard by the ears

Now you stop, look back on your life
How many have you crucified
Not giving someone a chance to be a friend
Because you listened to some one that lied

Inspired by and dedicated to a friend

God's Wonder

When men had given up on me
They had given me up for dead
As my body lay in a dormant state
My mind reflected on what the Bible said

Reflecting on what the Bible said
I remember Jonah in the belly of the whale
And Paul and Silas locked away
Singing and praying in some lonesome jail

I remembered God has always been good to me
I have been blessed, I could plainly see
I knew he still had work for me to do
And that he would deliver me

Yes I know I am God's wonder
Thinking about where he brought me from
When almost all hope was gone
I kept leaning on his everlasting arm

He said, just trust and believe in me
Be honest and sincere in prayer
If you should go down in the pits of hell
Fear not, I will be there

When I was flying high in my own little sky
Man made destruction forced me down
God said I still have work for you
And no ground can hold you down

After years of remolding and refining me
God finally set me free
Now I am a much greater and wiser man
Than I ever thought I could be

Like Job the world took away my passions
The things that meant so much to me
But God gave me back so much more
I will just praise him continually

Yes I am God's wonder
Look over my life and you will see
He brought me back from deaths door
Opened my heart, and mind and he delivered me

Dedicated to the volunteer fire Depatment of Mississippi

I See I Know I will

A blind man was tripping and stumbling
Trying to find his way home
No one to be his eyes, or lend a hand
He was in a dark world all alone

As he inched along with determination
He stumbled over a mass on the ground
As he tried to step over the mass
Something grabbed him, and he fell down

As the blind man got up to a sitting position
The ground mass began to talk
He asked the stumbler, what's wrong with you?
Can't you see that I can't walk?

The blind man didn't turn or blank
He said sir, please forgive me
I am a victim of this horrible war
I am blind and I can't see

The mass was so apologetic and sad
He said "daily I sit here and beg
I stepped on a land mind in this war
And lost both of my legs"

The blind man said I can't give up
But this is what I will do
If you will direct me where to go
I will do my best to carry you

So the blind man and the legless man
Traveled a mile or two each day
After a few days of travel
They found an armless man along the way

The armless man like the other two
Were thousands of miles away from home
He knew that he could help and needed help
For he too could not make it alone

The blind man and the legless man
Did the things that the armless man could not do
While the armless man sat quietly by
Until the job was through

The legless man and the armless man
Did the things that required the eyes
But kept the blind man well informed
So that nothing would be a surprise

The armless man and the blind man
Did the things that required the height of a man
They worked harmoniously together
Because the legless man could not stand

Their story resembled that of the lepers
They knew if they gave up they would surely die
They vowed with the help of God
They would give it their very best try

The blind man had a special possession
That he wore strapped to his back
He asked the legless man to open it
There was a Bible in his pack

The blind man said his Bible was his shield
His pillow many times in the fox holes
He knew if he lost that body
God, no matter what had his soul

The men remembered their childhood training
Each man had a scripture of his own
That they kept embedded in their heart
Far away and fully grown

The armless man was a scholar
He was well versed, and read
And the sightless man and the legless man
Listened as he quoted what the Bible said

They were especially fascinated
At the miracles Jesus done
They knew he could do the same for them
For he was the savior, he was God's son

With God's blessings they were rescued
With united efforts they made it home
Now the men truly had a story to tell
Each had a story of his own

The three men told their story
They felt it was a story the world should know
They had gone through a hell like a fiery furnace
Just like Shadrack, Meshack and abednago

No matter what your problems might be
There are two others that have it as bad as you
Merge and put it in God's hand
And see what miracle he will do for you

I wish you

I wish you a sun filled dawning
Fresh coffee aromas seeping into your room
Orange juice and toast after your shower
Smiles, kind words, instead of gloom

An unexpected phone call from an old friend
Bursting with energy that just won't stop
Green lights on, your whole day through
On your way to work or to shop

I wish you a day of many things to rejoice in
Short lines at the grocery store
A belly laugh at little annoying things
That normally would make you sore

To hear a song from your distant pass
Being played on the radio
And your keys being where you think they are
When ever you are ready to go

I wish you a day of happiness and perfection
That makes you know that God is looking down on you
That makes you feel real close to him
And that he approves of what you say and do

The feeling that you are very special to him
That makes you feel good, special and rare
Just because he is your loving father
And without a doubt you know that he cares

I wish you a day of peace and joy
And lots of time to find a friend
Even more time to get to know them
And time to pray that the friendship never ends

Plenty time to learn to love them
Share things that you will never regret
Spend the rest of your life relishing moments
And praying, them you will never forget

Dedicated to my mother MRS. ETHEL COLLINS GREEN, A woman among so many, she did so many wonderful things, for so many people of all races, creeds and colors. She was a friend to people of all ages. As far back as I can remember she was a devoted, dedicated woman of God. When you hear the phrase "take nothing and make something" they were talking about my mother. In every neighborhood we lived in you can still hear people speaking of the many wonderful things my mother done for anyone and everyone that crossed her path

Mama

Men lie and cheat to be president
Spend millions of dollars for that name
And forget the promises they made
Because to many that is prestige and a game

If they can't be president
To work in or around the white house
They will steal, backstab, murder and lie
Ducking and dodging just like a mouse

Being Governor is a fightable position
And too the pay is all right
Men and women a like, will forfeit their health
And spend many a sleepless nights

Being Mayor is just climbing the ladder
Keep back biting and you will soon be there
In high places and well noted
And many don't seen to care where

To some being Pope is a life long dream
Or being Bishop is doing God's will
Or is it just a title they desire
And another quota to fill

Being preacher, teacher or singer
A street sweeper or policeman
Will do whatever it takes to keep the job
That's something a lot of people can't understand

Still the greatest job on earth is mama
You don't have to connive, cajole or pay
Just be a God blessed woman
And God will send the blessing your way

I am not minimizing your jobs fathers
And I pray that you all are good dads
But thank you O God for Mamas
The best job title, anyone has ever had

Because Mamas births presidents and senators
Governors, king and queens and such
No matter how high you may rise
Somewhere, sometimes there was a Mama's touch

Though Mama is the least prestigious
And her job never change
The least paid, but has the hardest job
But that's nothing unusual or strange

Mama's works the longest, most impossible hours
Doing the things that mamas and daddies do
Not taking anything from you daddy's
But Mama sometimes has to be the daddy too

Only God works harder and longer than Mama
And only Jesus done something that mama's can't do
He too had a mama, lived and died
And rose for mama, and for me and you

Call her mother, mama or mommie
Call her mom or ma it's all the same
If you handle motherhood, and do it right
It's worth more than fortune and fame

Mama's hurts and cries too, for she is human
The same as me and you
But she is thankful, that God made her special
And prayer is what sees mamas through

To all Military personal of all wars, all over the world. We thank you for your protection, and we pray that all men will turn to God and find other ways to solve their differences, so that no more lives will ever have to be sacrificed. A very special thank you to my husband Sergeant James Terry Moore. God loves you and so do I.

I don't want to be here

Mama I don't want to be here
On this lonely Christmas morn
In this desolate war ridden country
The day when Jesus Christ was born

When I think of the Christmas's gone by
And Santa with toys in his sack
Here I am, I don't know where
With a rifle on my back

My Bible says honor all fathers and mothers
That I should not covet, lie or kill
Mama I don't want to be here
I can't believe I am doing God's will

It says love God with all my heart
And my neighbors and myself the same
But they sent me here to kill my neighbors
And I don't even know their names

Christmas is about loving and giving
About mankind, families and caring
I find my eyes filled with tears
When I look into these blank eyes staring

Nightly before I go to sleep
I get down on my knees and pray
That all wars will soon be over
And we can enjoy a happy Christmas day

I wonder if the heads of these countries
Knew God in the pardoning of their sin
Would they come together like human beings?
And bring these awful wars to an end

Mama I don't understand their language
And they cannot understand me
Chances are we could be friends
But this is how cruel a war can be

Mama it's early in the morning
You are checking the gifts under the tree
When you speak to God above the tree
Please tell him to watch over me

Mama pray for peace all over the world
And my friends as we huddle here in fear
Mama I don't want to be hurt or hurt anyone
Mama I don't want to be here

Ms. Georgia Street, one of the bravest women I have met in a long time. Though truly handicapped in many ways, she kept right on doing what she loved most. She worked tirelessly to educate the young untrained minds.

Georgia Street

She was born with a lust for knowledge
Preparing to give to the world as well as gain
Lived and learned to work real hard
She was on top of her terrain

She was a great asset to the job market
Learned a lot just being her best
Tackled every challenge that confronted her
Which prepared her for a greater test?

She was on her way onward and upward
Taking every dare slowly and by degrees
When cancer dealt her a fatal blow
She was struck with a life threatening disease

But with her in born determination and knowledge
She said to herself, oh no you can't quit
Her life and the things you want out of life
Just meant, you will have to work harder for it

Giving up, quitting, feeling sorry for herself
Was the easiest thing in this world to do?
Crawl if you have to, just go for it
As long as you get what you are due

When she could no longer work co-operartely
She still had to do her best
She started teaching the young eager minds
Preparing then for their scholastic tests

As the cancer progressively grew worst
That made it impossible for her to stand
She could no longer teach from the wall board
She decided to teach the next thing in demand

She could teach the computer from any angle
Young minds are always hungry to know
It is a tool that's a must for tomorrow
And they can use it where ever they go

In the work world she was a producer
Earning a living in a market creating greed
Today's job nets the average pay
But it fulfill a greater need

She says" I am not happy about my fall
But so grateful where I came land
My today's job is so much more rewarding
And is so greatly in demand

"Don't you sit down and feel sorry for yourself
If life deals you a terrible blow
It's really just fine tuning your map
For there are much greater places to go"

She feel so rewarded when she meet a youngster
That really has the computer at heart
She can teach them the computer from on to off
Or how to build one or take one apart

The future scientific minds that she is training
Maybe the ones to come up with the answer
To stop many diseases before they start
And someday find a cure for cancer

Daily she teaches from her wheel chair
Nightly she thanks and praises God too
Hoping that some of the eager minds she touch
Can prevent this from happening to you

Sure Georgia, just like everyone else
Took a moment for a pity party
But because her body was shutting down
Didn't stop her mind from being hale and hardy

Yes, she too went through the twenty questions
What did I do, why me, why now
But says, just as sure as my name is GEORGIA STREET
I am going to make it some way, some how

My Friend

Mabel Vernon Laider One of the nicest person
I have met in a long time

Mabel you came into my life, an angel
Like an answer to an honest prayer
At a time that I needed a friend the most
I looked and you were there

You are as loving and as comforting
As wind rustling through the leaves
You are as welcome and hoped for
As a cooling summer breeze

I love you because you are precious
To me you are a gift from God
You came during one of my down days
You were like a long awaited reward

I am always so happy to see you
But between visits your letters will do
One of the nicest days of my life
Was the day, that I first met you?

Mabel to me you are a living doll
Your struggles have made you caring and wise
You are a warm, loving and giving person
You are an angel in disguise

My Men

You ask, why I am no longer the life of that party
You want to know why now, I am always alone
True I am alone but not lonely
It's just that all of the good men are gone

Today's men are insanely jealous
Still they say, there is something wrong with me
Because I am too much woman for just one of them
That's why I always had to have three

I needed a man for all occasions
But that you don't understand
Because of my financial situation
I needed a money man

My money man worked all the time
Trying to please me any way he can
So that made the love making come up short
So I needed a honey man

Everyone of course has to eat
So naturally I needed a meat man
After each meal you want some desert
So I needed a sweet man on hand

The angels got jealous of me
And took them all away
But still I am not lonely
I have my memories of yesterday

My money man was wonderful
My honey man was never late
My meat man stood toe to toe to them all
And my sweet man was just great

Today's men are out there hunting
A lot of them won't even work
Many of them are in jail
And a whole lot of them are just jerks

So many males that we think are men
Are hopelessly, and insanely insecure
Some woman is hoping that they are men
And they themselves are not sure

So if a woman says no to you
Her quota might be filled, try to understand
With her meat man and her sweet man
And her honey and her money man.

Pig Pen to the Potter's House

I was whole and I was happy
But strange desires made me want to roam
Not sure of what happiness was
I foolishly wandered far away from home

It seemed in packing I forgot something
My teaching, self preservation and common sense
I was in a hurry to run barefoot
In the greener grass, on the other side of the fence

I ran head on into the bumps and bruises
O master potter, I could not wait
I could not flex my muscles, and be myself
Until I was on the other side of my father's gate

The world of stick and stones were waiting
But I was so cool I could not see
The pot holes and the traps that was in the world
That was lying there just waiting for me

I was having such a good time
I forgot about God, my father and mother
I was spreading my wares everywhere
Every one was my sisters and brothers

I was no longer stately and wholesome
Sin sought me from every side
I was stuck up with idle flattery
And filled with foolish pride

I was living in sand castles in the summer time
My friends were like the leaves on the trees
My house crashed at the first wind and wave
Friends disappeared at the first winter breeze

The world began to poke at me
I started to crack from pin sized holes
I had forgotten that I was made of clay
With the breath of God, a heart and soul

Thank you O potter there was enough godliness in me
To see that I was living in a pig pen
Feeling unloved and unworthy
Broken down by this world of sin

Thank God for my mothers and fathers prayers
Teaching me that everything God made was good, was fine
And if I asked, God will always love and protect me
He said, you and this world is mine

The world felt it had consumed and broken me
Had cast me into the pig pen
But I will arise and go back to the potter's house
And let him make me whole again

Thank you O God for loving me enough
To go with me through the pig pen
Then taking my battered and broken pieces
And making me whole again

Thank you O God you are the master potter
Showing me how to get away from the pig pen
With the Bible as your road map and welcome mat
Back to the potters house again

Lord if I only had known
I would not have had to go through the pig pen
But I guess that is our inquisitive nature
For we were born into a tempting world of sin

You just put your faith in the potter
If ever you are broken by sin
Leave that pig pen; go back to the potter's house
He will make you whole again

The Final Poem

When the final poem has been written
When all of the ink wells have dried
All of the poetic stories have been told
Or at least the poets will have tried

Their creating will rest for a minute
As they pass from life through the grave
As their poems will be song melodiously
As their verses are lifted in praise

Each poem will be a song of praise
As they lay their ink pens down
Their poems will be on the waves of time
As their souls are heaven bound

There they will meet the greatest poets
The authors and inspirer of all rhyme
Where we will sing our verses in praise to him
Of our trials, tribulations and times

There will be real stories to write of
Of streets paved with Gold
Flowing with milk and honey
And of wonders that have never been told

Their verses will be far sweeter
More savory than a vintage wine
More loving than the songs of Solomon
Growing more precious with every line

Uplifting as the Psalms of David
As protective as the staff and rod
As they dine in the midst of their enemies
While versing to the savior, our God

The Message or the Messenger

Why do you always call me on Thursday?
At nine o'clock for God's sakes
You don't have anything to talk about
You are trying to make me miss Rev. T.D. Jakes

Do you see how nicely he is dressed?
He is always clean shaven and precise
I just love watching him on TV
Because he is always so nice

And child I really get upset
And if you want to hear me hollow
Let something get in my way
To make me miss Rev. Crefflo Dollar

He too is a good one
And I can see him four or five times a day
I always watch him as long as I can
Until my soaps get in the way

I try to catch Rev. Eddie Long
And I just hate missing Rev. K. C. Price
Rev. Joel Olsteen, John Hagee, Joyce Meyers
They too are very nice

Ministers Marilyn Hickey, Juanita Bynum and Paula White
Just to name a few
I try to catch them when I can
Because I love watching them too

Rev. John Cherry, I. V. Hillard, Bill Winston
Ed Montgomery and their wives when I can
Their wives are out of sight dressers
I also watch them every now and then

I love Minister Benny Hinn and Oral Roberts
And I can't leave Rev. Billy Graham out
Come and see them with all of your infirmatives
You will leave healed without a doubt

Sister, tell me why do you have to watch them all?
What are they saying to you?
You say you can't remember their sermons
But if you miss them you don't know what to do

Friend I think you need to fast and pray
You need to find Jesus Christ for yourself
You will never get to heaven
Because of what's in someone else

Just forget about the messengers
And focus on the messages they bring
Because they too, just like you
Are waiting for Jesus Chris the king of kings

While you were watching all of those ministers
Did you learn anything about God or Jesus Christ the son?
About how God made a perfect world for you
And all of the wonderful things Jesus Christ have done

Just turn your TV off for a week
Stay out of the refrigerator thirty times a day
Then the messenger won't look so good to you
And you might hear what they have to say

Every once in a while you will hear them say
Find a nice Church in your neighborhood
Join, take your tithes, and fast, pray get involved
For wherever you are there is bad and good

Get involved in your neighborhood church
Hear what the messenger has to say
Then you won't care how the messengers attire look
You will be able to hear the messenger that day

Then you will start listening for the message
And reading your Bible to see what the scriptures has to say
You will get busy doing what God meant for you to do
And you won't have to watch TV everyday

Thelma Elizabeth Henderson

Lord I Thelma Elizabeth Henderson, doubted you
Lord I thought you didn't care
Many times I found myself wondering
If you had forgotten that I am here

Though the devil was with me constantly
Especially during my weakest hours
I forgot just how much you do love me
And about your amazing grace and power

Not realizing I was being selfishly self centered
My every thought was only of me
Until O Lord you stepped in and intervened
And drew me closer to thee

I had forgotten how you had blessed my life
The wonderful talent you had given me
The gift to help many unfortunate people
Still I wallowed in self pity

In my state of confusion I turned to my doctor
I needed someone, anyone to care
But all I really needed to do
Was to go to you in honest prayer

So I put my life in the doctor's hand
And I know he done the best he could
But neither I or the doctor knew
That our best really was no good

Then Lord you put me into a deep, deep sleep
And when the morning came
My trusty doctor couldn't wake me up
Though he was patting my hand and calling my name

My Loved ones came from near and far
They prayed for me, talked and held my hand
At that time you were showing me how much you cared
Though your ways I couldn't understand

The doctors, nurses, and loved ones came
And sat sadly by my bed
They all left one by one
Knowing that any day I would be dead

My doctor and the hospital gave up on me
They sent me to the nursing home
Just a stop over before the cemetery
So that I wouldn't have to die alone

While I lay there in that comatose state
I just know that you were there
Before the tragedy I was in doubt about you
But O Lord now I know you care

As the doctors and nurses and loved one
Came and went, shaking their head
Saying that any night might be my last
But thank you O Lord that is not what you said

When you decided that my night was over
You gently awakened me
Today I am a living testimony of your love
That the whole world can see

Dear Lord never again will I doubt you
Now I know without a shadow of a doubt
That you can take me through anything on this earth
And safely bring me out

So my brothers and sisters if you have any doubt
That God will ever leave or forget about you
I THELMA ELIZABETH HENDERSON is living proof
God is real and his promises are true

Dedicated to the first ladies of St Paul AME Church Of East Orange, New Jersey

Mrs. Donna Bell-Santucci

And

Mrs. Carol Kirkland Fubler

A Woman for every situation

Behind every great man there is a woman
Pushing his stroller wherever he goes
How far he will go, or how high he will rise
Only time and God knows

Over every man there is a woman
Saying son eat your vegetables please
If you want to grow up big and strong
Strong men start with their carrots and peas

In front of every man there is a woman
Pulling him along, helping him with his homework
Encouraging him to educate his mind
So that he won't grow up to be a jerk

For every man there is a woman down on her knees
Praying for him or finding his skates
Letting him know you must look high and low
To experience life, and find out what waits

Up under every man there is a woman
Trying to comfort him or rock him to sleep
Or wiping the tears from his eyes
Telling him that it's alright for a man to weep

For every polished, able man
There is a woman staying up late at night
Going over his notes, or ironing his shirts
To make sure that everything is right

For every man there is a woman
At some time or another praying for him
That he will stay on the straight and narrow
So that he won't be deterred by every whim

From the start there was a woman all around him
That first nine months of his life
Nourishing, protecting and praying for him
Hoping to prevent much stress and strife

When you hear, behind every great man there is a woman
Say yes, behind, in front, over under, around and through
And tell him if it had not been for a woman
There would be no you

My Song My Prayer

Lord let every word of my mouth
And the sincere thoughts of my heart
Be pleasing to your will and way
Each day before I start

Lord I pray the cries of my tongue
Be a pleasing supplication for a friend
Then too O Lord remember me
Before the blessings ends

Lord in my hours of trials
Please make it a time of care
For then O Lord I feel closest to you
In my sweet hour of prayer

Then I feel your rod and staff comforting me
Restoring my faith and trust
Knowing that you are always near
And what a friend I have in Jesus

I feel the pressure lifting
And forgiveness for the mistakes I have made
When I pour out my heart and soul to you
When my all on the altar is laid

Lord please except my thoughts and utterances
And steer me clear of all wrong
As I offer you my very best
O Lord in my prayer and in my song

As I try to love my friends and enemies
And show them how much you care
Lord perfect my thoughts, words and deeds
Through my song, please hear my prayer

Dedicated to Mr. J.D. Pike, a very dear friend of mine. He lived his life to the fullest. He lived and loved foolishly until he found Jesus Christ as his Lord and savior. Then he wanted the whole world to know that he had not even began to live, until he learned about Jesus Christ, the truth, the way, and the light.

My Testimony

I was a worm, I was a scum
One of the lowest things on earth
I should have been forced to experience the pain
That my mother bore for my birth

I was raised as a decent kid
I was taught that God was real
But as I became a man
I wanted something I could touch, taste and feel

I turned my back on God
Still, to me he was very good
He kept me alive, well and healthy
While I did every wrong thing, I could

I did whatever it took to please the world
To excel, make money to get by
I did just enough to fool the world
And keep money in my pocket to get high

Cigarettes, beer, wine and whiskey
That was okay for a start
But I needed something manly
Something to jump start the heart

I smoked reefer by the truck load
Used heron and cocaine
Angel dust, crack or whatever was available
I would try anything

I was married, but not a husband
Had children, but was not a dad
Why God didn't take his breath away
Because all of my thoughts and deeds were bad

I was a liar, a thief and a fornicator
Still God kept me in the palm of his hand
I must have been the world's greatest actor
Because my friends looked upon me as a man

I stole enough money day by day
To feed some small countries hungry
But I was stealing to buy drugs
My low life was all about me

Just as the Bible says
Train a child while they are young
Though they will go down to the gates of hell
They will turn back before too long

One day just like the prodigal son
I said, Lord I want to come home
He said drop the drugs, pick up my son
And leave the world alone

I got down on my knees, and started to pray
Confessing the many things that I did not understand
I told God I was a sinner, lower than dirt
But please forgive me; make me a husband, a man

That very instant he changed me
Drugs no longer had a hold of me
But being a liar and a phony so long
I had to go out and try and see

So once again I went out stealing
Buying from any dealer on any corner
Not realizing the God had freed me
And that Satan was no longer, my souls owner

I stopped drinking, drugging and fornicating
I realized that God had truly set me free
Now I have changed my song and dance
Now I am singing, nearer my God to thee

I no longer look down to hell
I lift my eyes up to the sky
God cleansed me and gave me Jesus Christ
And now I vow you will stay high

God will give you the house that he built for you
The mate that was in his plan
He will make you a father of many
He will make you his, he will make you new man

Each day I try to share my testimony with others
God is no respecter of persons
He will free you man, woman, boy or girl
Just drop the world, and to take up my son.

I shared my evil with many
I pray someday to make that right
Stop them from being blinded by enticing evils
To try Jesus the awesome light

Now that you have heard my sorry
Here is what you should do
Get on your knees and pray the sinner's prayer
Jesus Christ if waiting for your too.

Over the Rainbow

Sitting here feeling sorry for myself
Not sure of any particular reason why
Instead of climbing this rainbow that I am leaning on
Or at least giving it a try

It is so easy to wallow in self pity
Instead of doing as other do
Trying to find that pot of gold over the rainbow
That's just sitting there waiting for you

Somewhere over the rainbow
I have heard that all of my life
But no one thought to mention
All of the turmoils, obstacles and strife

For some reasons it seems that every time
I make up my mind to go over the rainbow
There is a hindrance in the way
Saying that this is not the time or the way to go

Then when I see the many that has gone over the rainbow
I decide to give it another try
If those little birds can make it over the rainbow
Then why in the world can't I

I am sick and tired of being sick and tired
I am going to give this rainbow another try
I have always wanted to soar close to heaven
And if I believe, I know that I can fly

Whether or not I find that pot of gold
If unlike the little birds I don't fly
I am going over that rainbow
For sure before I die

Every one is singing about over the rainbow
But I was using mine to prop up on
Everyone that want to go over the rainbow
It seems that they are already gone

Many say that now I am too old to go anywhere
My ship has come and is gone back out to sea
If it's not gong over the rainbow
That was not the ship for me

Now I am more determined
Bags packed, I am ready to go
Don't look for me sitting idly by
I am headed over the rainbow

People

Many think that people can be separated by color
Many think it's by how much money you've got
But forget about skin and money
And the differences are not a lot

Because no matter where you are from or are going
Whenever you are hungry you will eat
Whenever you have some place to go
If walking, you will have to use your feet

If the weather sudden changes
If you are catching a cold, you will sneeze
Or when the temperature starts to soar
You will welcome a cooling breeze

Everyone enjoys a belly laugh
At something funny or a very good joke
And if you want to live long and healthily
Don't be an abuser, a drinker and don't smoke

If someone hurts your feelings
That will always change a smile to a frown
If many times when you are walking
If you seriously trip, you will fall down

If you are cut you will bleed
Your blood is red the same as mine
If you lose something that is precious to you
That is something that you have to find

When you were born the doctor spanked you
Until you let out a whale of a cry
When you take time to look at the situation
There is really no difference in you and I

All of us were born toothless
Some of us without a bed to lie on
Some with all of the luxuries of this world
But when we die it will be all gone

If your color, money or education
Make you feel that you are greater than me
Live long enough for old age and senility to set in
Then where in the world will you be

If something is pleasant to the eye
You will take a second look
And if there is time and enough publicity
You will read a book

If someone gets hurt you are sad
At a funeral or a wedding we will cry
If we are blessed we will live long
But being born of a woman, you will die

So if you feel superior to someone
Remember that God made us all
Your color, money, or education will not help you
When it's your time to answer the call

Reason and Season

In Ecclesiastes you will find there is a time
For all things, there is a time and a season
Read your Bible daily and you will find
That Jesus is the reason and the season

You will find there is a season to be born
There also is a season to die
You will find between birth and death
There is a time to laugh and cry

There are reason and seasons for emotions
A season to go and a season to wait
A reason to love your friends and foes
And a time to hate the things God hate

As we all know there is a season to plant
And too there is a season to reap
In your youth is the season to work
The latter years is the season to sleep

Jesus Christ the son of God
Is the reason and the season
Was born on earth as the son of man
To reconnect God and man was the reason

Born in a stable in Bethlehem
During a cold dismal winter season
The world was awaiting a new king
Not knowing this was the season and the reason

In his season he went near and far
Teaching the teachers how to teach
He went into the temples and synagogues
Teaching the preachers how to preach

He chose twelve disciples to walk with
How to lift up his father and carry on
Knowing he was here for only a season
And for the reason he would soon be gone

He taught his disciples how to fish
To heal the sick and disabled at hand
How through faith make the lame to walk
How to become fishers of men

During his season he was disputed
They hung him upon a cross
That's the reason he came as a man
As the ransom for the lost

In Ecclesiastes we read about the seasons
There is a time to plant and reap as well
That Friday when they buried him in the tomb
He burst open the gates of hell

But early Easter Sunday morning
Was the season for the reason to rise?
To leave with us the holy ghost
Before going home beyond the skies

But that's not the end of the story
In our seasons we too were born and will die
The reason is to join him around the throne
For he lived and died to show us how

Satan wants his job back

Satan used to be a beautiful angel
Back when heaven was his home
When he had charge of many things in heaven
When he was around God's throne

He was one of God's executive officers
He had authority and power in his hand
But greed over took his common sense
He forgot that God was in command

He could delegate responsibility to other angels
Tell some angel to keep watch over the stars
Some he would tell to direct the choirs
But Satan forgot who he was

Satan began to get cocky
Started thinking he did not need God
He felt that he was doing all of the heavy work
So being the head was not so hard

Satan's ego had become so inflated
He became so jealous he didn't know what to do
His greed somehow made him forget
That God made Heaven, Earth, and made him too

Some of the angels, like the Israelites,
Saw Satan everyday
So they would go to Satan to gripe
When they had something to say

Anyone can put a bandage on a scrape
And that's just what Satan would do
But if the scrape became a sore
Satan knew, the answer, only God knew

Most of the angels didn't know
Just where the answers came from
As long as the problems were solved
They had forgotten about God's awaiting arms

Some of the angel's just like us
Forgets how much God cares
And all you ever have to do
Is take our problems to God in prayer

This too was a boost to Satan's ego
Many of the angels looked up to him
He had many thinking that he was their God
So he had control over them

Like many of us will follow our spouse
Money, alcohol, drugs or what ever make us feel good?
Instead of taking it to God in prayer
Like any God fearing being should

Because Satan was a big angel in heaven
He couldn't imagine all of the things God has to do
Like hearing and answering our every prayer
Taking care of the fish and the birds in the air

So Satan started his rebellion in heaven
Not even knowing what responsibility was all about
He insisted on a confrontation in heaven
And ended up being kicked out

Satan realized he had no where to go
Didn't know what he would do
Told God "If you will send me to earth
I will turn those people against you"

God being the greatest prodigal father
Decided to let his earthly children have a voice
He gave us every thing we would ever need
He even gave us a choice

So Satan came down to earth
With greed, hate, destruction and mayhem
Not realizing that he could not fool everyone
Trying to make us just like him

Now Satan misses his heavenly beauty
And the prestigious position he was in
Thought he could come down to earth
And he could be in charge again

Satan don't care about us at all
Nor about us going to hell
As long as he can keep us out of heaven
And out of his former position as well

If he could just get back into heaven
He would give anything to be head angel again
That's why he has to keep us out of heaven
Then maybe he can get his position back in the end

So forget about greed and hate
Beat Satan at his own game
Strive to make heaven your home
You be God's head angel in Jesus name

Yes Satan wants his former position
Would do anything to get it back
So you be careful what he does, good or bad
Don't be fooled by his act

Satan really don't care where you go
Nor does he care how badly you act
He thinks if he can keep every one out of heaven
He just might be able to get his position back

The Lie

I want to be just like Jesus
That is one of Christian's biggest lies
No body wants to live forever
But nobody wants to die

Today we want to born in a hospital
With loved ones all around
People frown on being born in a stable
And by no means on the ground

They frown on unwed mothers
They tell anyone they're a lie
If they say they were impregnated by God
That conversation, don't you even try

We want our parents to work in high places
We want them to always be the star
Nobody brags about, mediocre jobs
Like camel driver, fisherman, or carpenter

Turning the other cheek to the enemy
You have got to be out of your mind
Yes I want to be like Jesus
But I tell you, I am not that kind

I try not to yield to temptation
But if I fast a few days and nights
The mere conversation about food
Just might start a fight

Healing the sick and raising the dead
Is something I would try to do?
But if I thought that would get me killed
I would feel real sorry for you